S0-BRQ-652

WITHDRAWN

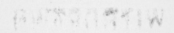

The
TWENTIETH-CENTURY
THEATRE

The TWENTIETH-CENTURY THEATRE

BY

FRANK VERNON , 1875 -

AUTHOR OF
" MODERN STAGE PRODUCTION "

WITH AN INTRODUCTION
BY
JOHN DRINKWATER

HOUGHTON MIFFLIN COMPANY
BOSTON AND NEW YORK

Printed in Great Britain

PN
2266
V4
1924

25-455

CONTENTS

CHAPTER   PAGE

Introduction   I

I. *Why Go to the Theatre?*   7

II. *The Nineties*   18

III. *The Writing on the Wall*   28

IV. *The First Years: I. "The Admirable Crichton" and the Court Theatre*   37

V. *The First Years: II. The Court Theatre*   47

VI. *John Brown's Soul*   57

VII. *One Theatre and the Other*   67

VIII. *Queen Horniman*   77

IX. *The Case of the One-Act Play*   87

X. *Mr Norman McKinnel*   98

XI. *The Censorship of Plays*   108

XII. *The Theatre of the Flappers*   118

XIII. *Post-War Tendencies*   128

XIV. *The Pressure of America*   138

XV. *The Theatre Resurgent*   148

v

49505

INTRODUCTION

"THE primary magic of the theatre is the magic of the spoken word," says Mr Vernon at the beginning of his little book, and at once we recognize a critic who knows what he is talking about. Mr Vernon's individual judgments may be provocative; they very often are. I myself, for example, think that he over-rates the most popular dramatist of the present moment, that he hardly pays due tribute to Mr Iden Payne's share in the work of the Gaiety Theatre, that he is rather less than handsome about Sir Arthur Pinero, and that his Honours List is perhaps a little arbitrary in including, shall we say?—no, we will not say—and omitting, for instance, Mr Nigel Playfair. I could wish also that Mr Vernon had sometimes allowed himself more room for exposition, as in his chapter on the one-act play, where the survey, by Mr Vernon's own standard, seems to be a little inadequate. Nor is our difference of opinion confined to in-dividual preferences. Having for some years taken a small part in the fight for the integrity of the provincial theatre, I have every sympathy with the refusal to admit London as the sole arbiter of taste, but I think Mr Vernon overdoes it when he says that " the life of the English provinces is so much larger a thing than the life of the home counties and London." It is no disloyalty to an old and deeply cherished association to say that, taken in the aggregate, this, intellectually and artistically, is not so.

These disagreements, however, leave me with the conviction that Mr Vernon has within a very small compass written the best book hitherto produced on a subject which he claims, and rightly, will take a very important place in the history of the English theatre. Literature without drama is useless in the theatre ; drama without literature may achieve some life there, but it is a life that has hardly any interest for people who have taken the trouble to become familiar with the significant art of the world. The only hope for a theatre that shall compete in intelligent appeal with the National Gallery and Everyman's Library and the Queen's Hall is a drama created by men who being masters of the " magic of the spoken word " have been encouraged to become also masters of stage life. This partnership between literature and the theatre, as is well known, had been in abeyance for nearly two hundred years, and was resumed only at the point where Mr Vernon's story begins.

That his book is well written I suppose every one will agree, but it has the further great advantage of being really well-informed. A work of this kind so often breaks down under the test of analysis at any point by the reader with inside information, but Mr Vernon's knowledge is always exact and first-hand. A sound general principle, direct information, and a forceful and witty style are imposing recommendations for a book, and Mr Vernon can claim them all. When he says a good thing it is always the better for having grown out of an ample and convincing context. " The new sort of play did develop a habit of beginning where the old sort left off " ; " There is need for something solid about which character can be characteristic " ; " The unexpected should occur in the words, not in the accessory " ; " War didn't damage only the drama ; it soiled the playhouses : it raped them. But the flappers didn't care ; nobody cared ; there was a War on, and why blame the flappers for caring nothing for decent tradition when Lord Rothermere wanted to turn the British Museum into offices for the Air Force ? " These are not happy phrases thrown off with journalistic ease ; in each case they clinch a balanced and well-conducted argument. We have to know a good deal about theatrical production and its history in the past twenty years, to know it as Mr Vernon knows it and is able to record it, before we can appreciate the perfectly timed significance of so simple a conclusion as, " The Court under Barker was naturalism *con brio* ; there were producers after Barker who left the *brio* out."

Mr Vernon's concern is chiefly with the pre-War twentieth-century theatre in England. His account of that is representative and responsible, and verdicts in future are not likely to differ materially from his own. His ruthlessly witty analysis of the War years in the theatre, again, is almost compensating joy for the flippant banality and cynicism that disgraced us in those days. His story of the post-War theatre is necessarily more fragmentary and told under greater difficulties. Having had no hand in the management of the Birmingham Repertory Theatre since 1918, I may without immodesty claim that a greater consideration might have been given to Mr Jackson's achievements there through a period when the Repertory spirit elsewhere in the provinces of England seems to have been defeated. Though it should perhaps be added that Mr Vernon does justly draw attention to the smaller enterprises throughout the country, of which not much has yet been heard in the world of fashion, even of intellectual fashion, but where in the hands of village and community players serious dramatic life has been fostered, and where perhaps

4

the hopes of to-day may most profitably look for encouragement.

Not that the London theatre is at present by any means the cause only for dejection. Hardly a week passes in which the intelligent playgoer (I mean the playgoer who when he wants to be amused declines to be put off with *Comic Cuts*, and who when he wants to be stimulated finds the psychology of the Thick Ear insufficiently subtle) cannot enjoy himself in one or another of the theatres. And perhaps one of the most hopeful signs of the post-War drama is a gradual shifting of interest from what may be called seedy to what may be called heroic life. The realism of the first years of the twentieth century, which found its apotheosis in the Manchester School, performed an invaluable service in restoring sincerity to the stage, in making the theatre, as Mr Vernon says, " a place not only for hacks but for artists." But there inevitably came a time when audiences, intelligent audiences, were a little enervated by plays in which they were provoked not so much to admiration as to a sympathetic condescension. Mr Vernon shows that he is not insensitive to the new needs when he writes, " There is no reason why drama should sit down, content with the naturalistic play, and should feel that it has no more worlds to conquer. The novel has been attacked by a disease called psycho-analysis, and is recovering from that malady ; drama has that warning before it, and, of course, the revolt from realism began long before the War." The fact is that the supreme exaltation of drama can only be achieved when the life presented is such that an audience finds itself straining in happy spiritual exercise up to its tragedy or achievement. It is not for nothing that the great dramatists of the world have always made the figures of their plays a little greater in stature than the common man. The great buffoons of comedy and the great victims of tragedy alike have always been something heroic in their measure, no matter in what environment they should move. And the post-War theatre in England whenever it has become significant has done so by respecting this tradition. Plays like *Outward Bound, Back to Methuselah, The Conquering Hero, Phœnix, The Lost Leader, John Fergusson, The Likes of Her*, and *The Bill of Divorcement*, very various in their defects and qualities, are alike in admitting an infusion of this heroic life, in attempting at least, each in its own way, the heights of a great argument. If the future should happily bring us splendid achievement in this kind, it will have to remember always with gratitude the foundations that were laid in the early days of the century when the Court Theatre was the wonder of the town, and half a dozen gallant enterprises in the provinces were starting their fires from Miss Horniman's torch. When, as will happen in a few years, those days have become a legend of the theatre, the new enthusiasts will be grateful for Mr Vernon's plain and authoritative record, just as we to-day are grateful to him for ordering our minds so well upon events that we have seen.

JOHN DRINKWATER

LONDON
May 1924

The
TWENTIETH-CENTURY THEATRE

CHAPTER I

Why Go to the Theatre?

A POINT to be made at the beginning is that there are two theatres, the theatre of drama and the theatre of musical comedy and revue ; and if progress is in question, the development of the lighter stage, both technically and socially, is probably a more surprising phenomenon of the last thirty years than the development of serious drama. It has reacted upon serious drama, it has caused drama, in sheer self-defence, to extend itself upward ; the pressure from below has squeezed out of serious drama a superior vintage, and the more the two are separated the better for the higher artistic interests of the theatre. They don't mix.

More is to be said later about that ; let it pass, for the moment, that there are two distinct theatres, that a strongly marked distinction between them is to the advantage of both, but that the chief concern of these pages is with the theatre of drama.

The query "Why go to the theatre?" shall be answered brutally and candidly in the case of the theatre of revue. The answer is that people go for general reasons applicable to both theatres and for the particular object of receiving a tonic to their animal spirits. Ask why they go to a revue, and the reply hypocritically may be, "Because I like light music"; it may silently be a wink, or it may frankly be the acknowledgment that they go to procure the emotions of mixed bathing in a place where those emotions are not corrected by cold water. Revue sketches frequently reach a high standard of worldly-wise wit; they are able dramatizations of smoking-room stories; they are even sometimes able little tragedies, to point a piquant contrast; but physical audacity (which means as near an approach to nudity as the Censor will allow) is the backbone of revue, and usually it is a very naked spine. Musical comedy keeps to a higher standard, and it is difficult in many cases to determine where light opera ends and where musical comedy begins; tunefulness, at any rate, is the *clou* of musical comedy, though without a comedian of infectious high spirits no musical comedy can hope to succeed, and the embarrassed theatre-goer who has recourse to a wink when asked why he goes to a revue could justly assert that light music and the engaging patter of some wizard of nonsense are the magnets which draw him to musical comedy.

8

Now the danger of idealists is that they are people with too high an opinion of human nature, and the charge the idealist of the drama brings against his fellow-men is that the shallow creatures will persist in going to the theatre as ' a night out.' Heaven forfend solemn playgoing! The theatre is necessarily a night out because one does not arrive inside a theatre by staying at home, and while nobody but a bigot objects to occasional theatre nights which are care-free jollifications, there is every reason why every theatre night should not be a revue night. Revues, really, need defence; and we haven't to-day a Charles Lamb to defend them as he defended Restoration drama. But Cloudcuckoo-land is a perilous everyday, or every night, resort, and even Lamb himself put it, " It is good *now and then* for a dream-while or so to imagine a world with no meddling restrictions, the Utopia of gallantry where pleasure is duty and the manners perfect freedom." Much virtue in that " now and then." And the law of supply and demand actually settles the question against the stern moralists; there are not enough revues for every night because they are not demanded every night, and the not-too-stern moralist can find a sane satisfaction there and a malicious satisfaction in the frequenting of the Bankruptcy Court by producers who have vainly imagined that the demand for revue is infinite and undiscriminating.

The retort to the idealist who protests that people regard the theatre as a night out is, " Which night ? " and it is the other nights, nights neither of musical comedy nor of revue, as to which the question is now put, " Why go to the theatre ? " The temptations to stay at home and the temptations, alternatively, to go anywhere but to the theatre are so strong as to lead to the conclusion that playgoing survives in the face of multiplied competition because it has behind it the sentiment that the theatre is a joyous place. And if the idealist is pleased to take exception to that sentiment he is puritan in the blackest sense of the word and an enemy to his own ideals, because without the feeling that the theatre is joyous the theatre would cease to exist, and the value of ideals about a non-existing theatre is below zero.

The theatre survives because it is the best means of satisfying human desire for the emotions received from witnessing drama. It is not the only means ; that is where competition comes in ; and sport is the strongest competitor of the theatre, weakened only by the fact that most, but not all, spectacular sports must be seen in daylight. Boxing, for instance, is crude drama which as entertainment competes directly by taking place in the evening. The leisured conflicts of the cricket-field and the more concentrated conflicts of football and tennis are less direct but none the less strong competitors ;

so is the drama of the racecourse and (again an evening event) the drama of the bridge-table. The other chief competitors are print and the kinema, the drama of fiction and the drama of photographs, the one strongly tempting to stay by the fireside, the other offering on easy terms a pale and reduced substitute for the night out at the theatre. It may seem, in some of these examples, that the word 'drama' is misapplied; but the sense of conflict, and the emotions to which it gives rise, are present in all sporting contests; the objectives of the novel and the film are the same as the objectives of the play, and man is not infinitely emotional nor (if he were) infinitely at leisure. It is possible for him to get drama to the point of his personal saturation without undergoing the trouble and expense of going to the theatre for it. A 'best-seller' from the library or a shilling seat in a kinema are cheap substitutes for the high and puissant emotions of the theatre, and by the time one has finished thinking of gramophones and radio, of winter evenings and the disinclination to turn out for anything else than dancing, of summer evenings and daylight-saving combined with the passions for golf and tennis, it becomes surprising that the theatre, unique instrument for arousing and satisfying emotion as it is, should retain its place secure among the varied counter-attractions of modern life.

The theatre wins over the most gripping novel because reading is a private and playgoing a public pleasure. We are gregarious, and the pleasure we derive from the intervals between the acts in the theatre results from the evidence they afford us of a community with our fellow-men. That is not a quality peculiar to the theatre, but it is felt less in the darkened kinema or in the lighted concert-hall than during the intervals between the acts, when each fall of the curtain and each turning up of the house lights brings to an audience a fresh realization of itself as audience. Nothing is more wrong-headed than to write a play without a break, like *Getting Married*, and to ignore the human value of intervals. In practice, *Getting Married* is broken up, and its author's discovery that " the Greek form is inevitable when drama reaches a certain point in poetic and intellectual evolution " belongs to a future adumbrated, perhaps, in the bloodless Utopia of *Back to Methuselah*, but not likely to be reached by audiences of our time, who are unpoetic and unintellectual to the point of appreciating the social geniality of intervals.

But to speak first of intervals is to put the cart before the horse ; if they are not intervals between acts which have been worth listening to, they are more likely to be disgruntled periods when men wonder why they came to the theatre, and determine to resist feminine pressure to come again, than pleasant relaxations from emotional thrills. We go to the theatre, then, because drama in the theatre is drama in uniquely satisfying form ; the silent physical drama of sport or of the kinema and the second-hand drama of printed fiction dwindle to insignificance before the lure of the spoken word. The flesh-and-blood speaker of the audible word, the story told and the conflict fought, æsthetically, emotionally, humorously, by speaker against speaker —these are the compelling and essential attributes of the permanent theatre. If one were to sub-divide the actor's accomplishments, placing them in order of importance, it is certain that the art of elocution must come first, because the primary magic of the theatre is the magic of the spoken word.

The serious theatre survives by deserving to survive, by becoming increasingly distinguishable from the lighter forms of entertainment, by not imitating in emptiness of content the deliberate plotlessness of musical comedy or the clever flip-pancy of revue, but by standing firmly to its first principle of the spoken word in association with dramatic action. Pantomime (wordless plays) and spectacle for the sake of spectacle are by-blows of the theatre ; they are actual perversities because they are traitors to the sovereignty of words. The efficiency of musical comedy and revue is welcomed because it is one of the motives which drives the upper theatre upward. That theatre lapses when

13

it seeks, by spectacle or ballet, to borrow from the
theatre of revue ; it encourages some of its numerous
outside competitors when it discourages the spoken
word and forgets that, of all its arts, the art of
elocution is the first ; and some vehemence in re-
asserting the importance of lines well written to
be well spoken is not merely pardonable but urgent,
lest drama become a lost wanderer in the wilderness
of ' stagecraft.'

The advantages the theatre has over the kinema
are the bodily presence and the spoken word of
the actor ; the human voice, managed by an
elocutionary artist, gives an exquisite and exciting
pleasure beside which the most brilliant book is
dull. But the actor's is an interpretative act. He
is in the hands of the man behind, and if the quality
of a play is poor and if the dialogue is uninspired
the most beautiful and skilled speech will be of no
avail. It is, therefore, of playwrights rather than
of actors, of the unseen cause rather than the seen
and heard effect, that one must chiefly write in
celebrating and in criticizing the theatre of the
twentieth century ; but (authors won't like to hear
it) it is the actor and the actress, the visible and
audible interpreters of the play, who are the cause
of filled theatres. Out of sight, out of mind : that
is the case with theatre audiences and writers of
plays. The actor is seen and the actor is heard
(the condemned fools who are not heard don't

merit the name of actor), and people go to the theatre to see and to hear actors.

The natural predisposition to vanity of actors will, it is earnestly hoped, not be encouraged by these statements. On the contrary, to redress the balance, actors are the instruments of authors, and even audiences are not utterly unaware that plays have creators and vary in quality with the quality of their creators. Audiences are aware of Sir James Barrie, who draws them to the theatre as potently as Sir Gerald du Maurier himself. They are aware of Bernard Shaw, who is the author-idol of Repertory, and specialized audiences are responsive to some, but to very few, other authors. Nevertheless, since one hopes to go below the surface, authors must receive more attention than actors in any inquiry into the state of the theatre. Their work precedes the actor's ; their work, if it is good, lives after the individual actor and after its creator himself. The spoken word must be a good word, and the art of elocution is first only of the *actor's* arts : before his art comes the art of the author. Besides, it happens that English plays of the twentieth century are, as plays, very much greater than English acting, as acting. A pretty controversy might be suggested by asking how many good plays have been let down by bad acting compared with the number of bad plays which have been saved by good acting. (It is probably fifty of the first to one of the second, but there shall be no dogmatizing about it.) The point is that these good words, which when well spoken are the salvation of the theatre, are supplied to actors by authors, and that if audiences are not inquisitive about causes they are sensitive to results.

With the exception of Barrie, Shaw, and Galsworthy, no author's name draws anything appreciable to the box-office. Mention to a hesitating playgoer that a play is by Monckton Hoffe or by Harold Brighouse or by Macdonald Hastings, and he will look blank and then ask brightly, " Who is in it ? " No, people don't consciously go to the theatre because of authors ; they are capable— people who have had no opportunity of meeting an actress in private life—of saying, " I do like Miss X. She's always so witty." Miss X takes them into the theatre, not Messrs A, B, and C, who write the witty lines she has spoken in their plays : that is the stock example of the sensitiveness of audiences to results and of their insensibility to causes. The man who photographed the film has his name thrown on the screen, the author of a play has his name on the programme, and audiences care as little about the one as about the other.

The sum is that the ear beats the eye in the theatre proper ; in the other theatre (which shall

not be called improper), in the theatre of light entertainment, the eye beats the ear. The advance of the
serious theatre is due, first of all, to recognition of
the importance of words. Why do people go to
the theatre ? They go to hear speakers in acting
plays.

CHAPTER II
The Nineties

IN practice it is unfortunately unsafe to trust the schools of elocution and to assume that the right words will be rightly spoken, but in theory competent elocution must be taken for granted, and leave must be taken here to concentrate upon the right words, making the admittedly large assumption that the right words will not be wronged by perverse intonations or by that black crime of the modern theatre, inaudibility.

The right words! If we knew them when we saw them in advance of production, in typescript, there would be no failures, but the play-words with which we are now dealing are not prospective, but past; they have been tested by production, they exist in the printed form, and what is here to be said about them may in some degree be matter of opinion, but is not matter of speculative opinion. But some things are beyond argument, and it is not to be questioned that since the Elizabethan outburst no such number of the right play-words has ever been written and spoken in England as during the pre-War years of the twentieth century.

Pinero was in the eighties (the day of his farces), or else it was the day of his derivative problem plays and of the delightful *Trelawny*; it was certainly not in the twentieth century. With him, Mr Henry Arthur Jones. *The Middleman* is great melodrama, *The Liars* a notable, four-square, upstanding comedy that puts some overpraised contemporary trivialities to shame. But the twentieth century counts Mr Jones out.

One is conscious of the brutality of saying that still living playwrights have been without effective influence on their time for more than twenty years. Better, with their great fellow of the nineties, Oscar Wilde, to have died? But decidedly not. *His House in Order* is there to answer in this century for Pinero, and *Mrs Dane's Defence* and the jolly comedy of *Dolly Reforming Herself* for Jones. And the virtual disappearance of their type of plays is due partly to the Three Musketeers of the nineties, Shaw, Archer, and Grein, but very much more to the facts, the social and political influences which made inevitable the revolt against the play well made as to shape but empty as to democratic significance.

It is not to be known whether the Fabian movement led Shaw to the theatre or whether Shaw led the Fabian movement there, but the Fabians in the theatre and the Stage Society on Sunday nights were the spearhead of a movement much wider than Fabianism or the specialized playgoing of the *intelligentsia*. It was the movement set up by the Education Act of 1870, fortified in its critical assaults upon the masterly remoteness from life of that normal theatre of the nineties by various Continental influences such as Ibsen, the coming to England of translations of the Russian novelists, the French school of realism, and the native English revolt—expressed in such differing forms as *The Yellow Book*, *Esther Waters*, the Employers' Liability Act, the Committee on Sweating, Mr John Burns and the dock strike of 1889, Aubrey Beardsley, the Wilde of *The Soul of Man*, Swinburne, George Gissing, and women riding bicycles—the revolt against the smug self-satisfaction of "All's right with the world," and the questioning of a social order which appears in the plays of the typical playwrights of the nineties to be unquestionable. In that attitude to life the theatre was an obstinate conservative; no wonder Shaw shocked them, no wonder that theatrical reactionaries (applauders of the theatre of the nineties still exist and still function in the Press) deplore the dramatic revolution which made the great age of modern British drama in the years between the Boer War and the Great War. For the nineties had extraordinarily much that was vivid, exuberant, and urgently alive. In retrospect it is difficult to use the phrase *fin de siècle*, to suggest weary men

some comedy, tragedy, and character to be perceived in the ordinary man. We haven't guillotined
the aristocrats off the stage, but the New Drama
has very nearly scaled down the proportion of titles
on the stage to a reasonably lifelike limit. "The
poor are God's people," said Meredith, and though
his novels don't show that he made them distinctively his people (leaving that to Dickens and
to Hardy), it is certain that the poor, rather than
the titled and the secure, were the people of the
New Drama. At last the theatre had got into
contact with life, where, curiously enough, most
people have neither titles nor security ; and plays
were being written about the people who went to
see them.

CHAPTER III

The Writing on the Wall

MUCH could be made, but too much must not be made, of the idyllic economics of the theatre when the New Drama was in swaddling-clothes. In those days gross receipts of £800 a week led if not to ecstasy at least to contentment, while in these days gross receipts of £1500 a week are necessary to achieve the same result. Retrospectively considered, the New Drama rose in an economic paradise, but the same state of bliss and the same unconsciousness of that state surrounded all theatrical enterprise of that time. The post-War problem is the attracting of a minimum of £1500 a week to the box-office; the pre-War problem was the attracting of £800 a week; and while the drama in possession (derivatives of Dumas, like *Zenda, Beaucaire, If I were King*; derivatives of Ibsen, like *Tanqueray*, and so on; and derivatives of Robertson) easily reached and topped the essential £800, the attacking drama failed to attract that sum.

The drawing power of *Arms and the Man* at the old Avenue Theatre in 1894 is stated by Mr Shaw to have been £23 2s. 5d. per performance, or a who began to lose money gloriously in the theatre at the Avenue in the nineties.

About this time it began to dawn on English consciousness that there were other forces than Ibsen in Continental drama and other plays than Palais Royal farces. The adaptation of the *boulevard* play we have always had with us, and it is illuminating to find an American, Professor Phelps, writing of Capus, Donnay, Bataille, Lavedan, De Flers, and Caillavet that, " in comparison with the best British dramatists of to-day, they are like children playing with blocks in the same room with authors writing books." The modern Frenchmen are without influence in England. Brieux arrived in England because Shaw patronized him, and Rostand, a giant, wrote verse which both suffered in translation and made no breach in the modern British resolve to use prose drama as its medium of expression.

Maeterlinck had, indeed, some influence, D'Annunzio not much beyond the literary influence of the Arthur Symons translation of *Francesca da Rimini*, but the Germans Hauptmann and Sudermann, because they seemed on the whole out for much the same as the English school, were listened to and heeded. Except for *Magda*, that rather dreary play, they were listened to in print rather than on the stage ; but Hauptmann's *Hannale* played a part in the development of the

31

modern dream-play, and his *The Weavers* had something to say about realism. So had Tolstoy's *Powers of Darkness* and *Fruits of Culture* and Gorky's *The Lower Depths*. The influence of Tchekov is visible enough in the short stories of Katharine Mansfield and other moderns, but the influence of Tchekov's plays is not very palpable, even though Shaw calls *Heartbreak House* a "fantasia in the Russian manner." And the modern Italians and Spaniards are only just now reaching us, like the Czecho-Slovaks, *via* America.

On the whole, at the beginning of our period in the nineties the significant Continentals were being translated and printed rather than translated and acted, except at a few special performances in the afternoon or on Sunday nights. But the influence neither of the Sunday night (meaning at this time almost exclusively the Stage Society) nor of print is to be ignored. There was an outburst of good writing about the awakening theatre and growing critical impatience with the old—not so much from the professional critics, who largely took their lead from Clement Scott, as from writers in the reviews, who represented much better than the old professional critic the new demand for educated and lifelike drama. The printing of plays became a feature; tribute is due in this regard to the late William Heinemann, who set the example, followed later by others, among whom

32

Messrs Duckworth and Messrs Sidgwick and Jackson were prominent, with the delectable " Repertory Series " of Gowans and Gray earning a special mark afterward. The standards of dramatic criticism were revolutionized not only in such organs as the *Saturday Review*, where a Max Beerbohm followed a G. B. S., but in the daily papers. The *Star* gave Mr Walkley leave to speak his mind, Mr E. F. Spence was urbanely devastating in the *Westminster Gazette*, and the erudite zestfulness of Mr C. E. Montague in the *Manchester Guardian* set a new standard for the provinces and helped to create that provincial self-reliance which found expression in the Repertory theatres.

It resulted from this stir, for which the modern term is 'propaganda,' that serious literary artists began to change their minds about the theatre. They had thought of it as something ' inevitable ' (to use Matthew Arnold's word), but contemptible ; they thought of it as Mr Wells thought of it when he wrote *Kipps* and invented the playwright Chitterlow and his play *The Pestered Butterfly*— " much more legitimate than *The Wild Duck* "— with its *scène à faire* about a man with a beetle dropped down his back. Or else they yearned for the theatre as Henry James yearned and laboured massively but unsuccessfully to write a play—a strange failure in one who could write the dramatic dialogue of *The Turn of the Screw*. The construc-

C

tion, the architectural qualities, and the plotfulness of Thomas Hardy's novels seemed to prove him a dramatist at will, but would he ? No, he wrote *The Dynasts*, and *The Dynasts* is tremendous, but it isn't for the theatre. If it isn't the greatest closet-play in the world it makes a strong bid for that place, but a closet-play is a no-play, written for performance in the mind of the reader. The pity is that few stage-plays have so many right words as *The Dynasts* ; the abridged, mangled version which *has* been produced on the stage proves how wonderful a stage-play Hardy might have written had he but cared ! The case of Mr George Moore is different ; the will to write for the stage seems to be there, and some constructive power is evident, but what is lacking is the gift (not, one imagines, to be acquired) of writing stage-dialogue. It is all very distinguished, but it doesn't speak. There were failures, like James and Mr Moore, among the triers, but the new phenomenon was that there were triers of quality at all and that an attitude of despair or simply of contempt toward the theatre as a medium of expression was passing. The first-rate minds of the day were no longer being revolted by, they were being attracted toward, the theatre whose 'inevitability,' they began to perceive, was not only for hacks but for artists. Behind them social democracy pressed for expression—the death of Dukedom rather than the celebration of dukes—and the exponents of the social drama were undergoing their apprenticeship. Mostly they did their prentice work in private. It was later that the Repertory Theatre gave us the edifying spectacle of young playwrights— Stanley Houghton is the example—doing their prentice work in public. The earlier men had not his advantage of being able to see their first plays publicly performed, though lately Mr Milne has certainly been allowed to use the public stage as his practice-ground. But the writing on the wall was faint to the end of the nineties. Shaw was visible, as a *coterie* playwright, and Barrie as the sentimentalist of *The Professor's Love Story* and as the Kailyarder of *The Little Minister*, but, generally, it was the darkest hour before the dawn, and he would have been a very sanguine prophet who could have foretold, out of the evidence in sight, such a dramatic renascence as was about to come. There was, as we have seen, plenty of cause for a renascence, but the accomplishment far transcended its causes. If the pendulum was bound to swing, it was certainly not bound to swing so high ; it was not bound to give us, it was bountiful and amazing that it did give us, besides the mature Shaw and the mature Barrie, dramatists like Barker, Hankin, Masefield, Galsworthy, Synge, Houghton, Brighouse, and Chapin. An upward leap from the normal stuff of the nineties was inevitable—the

35

alternative was the death of the theatre—but the mass and variety of the new drama made it a thing to marvel at. A single play, *The Silver Box*, by a till then unheard-of playwright caused astonishment, even in the midst of the astonishing Court Theatre season; but those were comparatively early days, and the faculty of being astonished by good plays was blunted as good play succeeded good play. We can stand back a little to-day, we can see the whole outpouring of that time a little in perspective, and we can be astonished the more at this distance by the excellence and the diversity of the plays put forth by the galaxy of dramatists who belonged distinctively to the pre-War period of the twentieth century. Let there be no mistake about it : dramatically those were illustrious years.

CHAPTER IV

The First Years: I. "The Admirable Crichton" and the Court Theatre

IN the first years of this century British drama meant drama in London. There were pioneers like Miss Janet Achurch and Mr Harold V. Neilson, who stubbornly persisted in educating the English provinces up to an appreciation of *Candida*, *Captain Brassbound's Conversion*, and even *The Admirable Bashville*; and in 1899 Mr Murray Carson had performed *The Devil's Disciple* at Kennington. It all counted, and it was all a little heroic, but (whatever may have been happening to Shaw's plays in America and in Germany) Bernard Shaw remained practically a dramatic outcast from London until 1907, and Barrie, with *The Admirable Crichton* in 1903, is the opener of the great period. It is convenient to say that pre-War twentieth-century drama began in 1903 with *The Admirable Crichton*, and ended, surviving into the War, with *Hobson's Choice* in 1916. The pre-War standards lasted so far into the War, just as the War standards outlasted the Armistice, and the two plays named definitely usher in and definitely close a period, historic already, of British drama.

Quality Street belongs to the same year, 1903, and its revival in 1921 gives furiously to think, too, of its quality when compared with the contemporary plays of 1921. The plays of this period *do* revive, with disturbing results to some valuations of present-day drama, and the plays of the nineties (*Tanqueray* is, perhaps, an exception, and so are the rule-breakers Barrie and Shaw) do not revive. Still, *Quality Street* is not more than charming; *The Admirable Crichton* is solid food from beginning to its original end, which, by some error of judgment, Barrie altered from a perfect irony to an imperfect sentimentality for the 1919 revival. That was an attempt to leave the audience satisfied at the end of *Crichton*, to soothe them against the very thought which it is the business of this play to arouse through exquisite emotion. May the first ending be restored, and may future revivals end to unsatisfied, thoughtful audiences, not to audiences made thought-free by a trick solution! There is no solution to *Crichton* so long as this civilization lasts—that is its tragedy; and its significance at the opening of this period was that here was a moving play, masterly in its mingling of fantasy and realism, its pitting of natural against civilized conditions, its technical balance between the delicately chosen word and the fastidiously invented ocular effect,

38

which was supremely effective at once as a piece of the theatre and as social criticism. The thing which they doubted could be done was done; the theatre was triumphantly demonstrated to be a place where the bases of our civilization could be discussed to full houses.

It is to be doubted if the significance of *Crichton* was perceived; something of the fate of pioneers attaches itself to this play. It was successful, but Barrie has had larger successes with smaller plays. Perhaps that is to say that its significance *was* perceived and hated, and that its success was due to what it had in it flattering to the conventions of Society. It could have been written bitterly, defiantly, with a new last act completely carrying out the passing demobilization sentiment which Barrie half-heartedly acknowledged in the 1919 ending, and it would have gained as man... to and lost as truth. It could have been an assault on the structure of Society, and it is ironic comedy which accepts that structure. The portent was that a dramatist who was not, like Shaw, an avowed rebel had dared in a West End theatre to raise questions about the organization of Society. Barrie did not offer any panacea in reply to the questions he raised; he pointed to their existence, and, being a dramatist and not a propagandist, he left it at that. It is the smaller writers of the period, it is especially the women writers, who took the view that their business was not merely to state cases, but to propose remedies. Propaganda occurs with more discretion in Miss Hamilton's *Diana of Dobson's* than in her *Just to Get Married*, while Miss Robins' *Votes for Women* and Mrs Lyttleton's *Warp and Woof* are direct propaganda plays.

To write propaganda plays is to misread the lesson of *The Admirable Crichton*. Social criticism was doubtless a leading motive of the new drama ; because it was a drama which accurately reflected its times it could not help but be a social drama, and what there was of shrillness in its note of social criticism was due to its own bounding youth, to reaction from the obstinately uncritical drama which preceded it, and to the exuberance of its delight at finding the theatre open at last to the expression of social discontent. But it is to be emphasized that direct propaganda plays were exceptional, and that *The Silver Box*, *Strife*, and *Justice* are true children of *The Admirable Crichton* in that they raise questions about social problems and leave audiences to draw their own conclusions. Incidentally, one must not be taken as saying that the women playwrights were, in general, propagandists. There is no touch of propaganda in the greatest play by a woman of this time, *Rutherford and Son*, by Miss Githa Sowerby, nor in that exact and realistic statement of the city clerk's problem, *Chains*, by Miss Baker. The early and the late

40

is that the Court Theatre season of modern drama
began at the Lyric Theatre with Euripides made
actable for the English by Gilbert Murray; it
may have begun to begin when Mr Granville
Barker produced *Two Gentlemen of Verona* for Mr
J. H. Leigh at the Court, but Mr Barker's production of the *Hippolytus* was not only the first real
eye-opener to his quality as producer, but a true
preliminary to the Court *matinées*, which, after
beginning with *Candida*, went on to repeat the
Lyric performances of the *Hippolytus*. *The Trojan
Women* and the *Electra* in Gilbert Murray versions
were done later on, and if, then, *The Trojan Women*
hadn't the startling modernity—the topicality—it
had when seen during the War, nobody will deny
that Greek tragedy in Gilbert Murray translations
is modern. These plays are enough by themselves
(and they were not by themselves) to rebut the
charge that modern drama eschews poetry. Gilbert
Murray was not for pedants, but for Everyman, and
the service he rendered to English-speaking readers
was great, but greater still the service he did by
making Greek tragedy at home on the English
stage.

Partly the Court Theatre was the heir of the
nineties—the gathering together of plays already
written which the new spirit had evoked—and
partly it was the cause of plays being written; but
its main heritage was the mature Bernard Shaw in

assured possession of his astonishing powers as a dramatist, and before he became too much assured. *John Bull's Other Island*, *Major Barbara*, *Man and Superman*, and *The Doctor's Dilemma* were all first produced at the Court, with revivals of *Candida*, *You Never Can Tell*, *The Philanderer*, and *Captain Brassbound's Conversion*. The Court was the Shaw Theatre, with intelligent interruptions. It is probable that two later plays by Shaw, *Fanny's First Play* and *Pygmalion*, have enjoyed more popularity than any of the Court plays, though *You Never Can Tell* must run them fairly closely; but one feels that the Court had Shaw at his best, his most characteristically 'Shavian' period, with the three plays *John Bull's Other Island*, *Major Barbara*, and *Man and Superman*. All Shaw, of course, appeals more to the ear than to the eye, but never, not even in *Heartbreak House*, does the playwright in him forget the need for ocular shock-tactics. *Arms and the Man*, *Cæsar and Cleopatra*, *Androcles and the Lion*, and *The Devil's Disciple* make large and deliberate use of the pictorial; in a play like *Major Barbara* the pictorial is subdued to a big drum, Salvation Army uniforms, and the setting of the last act; and Shaw calls the whole affair " a discussion." Well, there have not been many acts written as dramatic as the second act of the ' discussion,' *Major Barbara*. It has been said that no great play exists without its discussion, and that the last act is the place for

the discussion. Shaw certainly discusses, and ultra-
modern impatience with words is capable of finding a something tedious in the last-act discussion
of, for instance, *Major Barbara*. Shaw does ask a
modern audience to leave its War neurosis at home
and to extend itself a little in the exercise of
using its ears ; he asks for an audience untired by
tennis, and if they can't to-day savour the poetry
of Keegan and the comedy of Broadbent and the
passion of Major Barbara, then audiences have
degenerated, and it is they and not the Shaw
masterpieces that are less than they were. *Getting
Married does* try an audience unreasonably severely ;
Man and Superman does not.

It may be put that in about half his plays Shaw
is Everyman's dramatist and that in the other half
he is distinctively the dramatist of the man who
listens. *Arms and the Man* is simply a well-made
play ; it relies not on wit or mental gymnastics, but
on a simple idea plus technique which seizes and
holds attention. Later, Shaw took a higher opinion
of his audiences ; he presumed that they would
listen to the right words and he gave them the
right words, occasionally breaking out of instead of
being confined by the shape of his plays. He took
liberties in the name of wit which his imitators take
without reason. Shaw could do that because he
is essentially a playwright and his liberties ' come
off ' ; he is not, as the old school tried to say, an

iconoclast misusing the theatre for his own ends, but a dramatist to his finger-tips. His words are the right words, and the fair comment on that is that it is possible to have too much of a good thing; his ideas were irrepressible, and he permitted himself to express them in plays which already carried their full weight of ideas. The trouble resulting from this was not so much the trouble of Shaw, but of weaker men who hadn't his ideas, and who imagined that because Shaw's plays weren't always shapely therefore shapelessness made great plays. Shaw's plays are great, less some shapelessness; theirs were shapeless without greatness. Shaw happens to be first a great dramatist and second the boldest, most fruitful, most original thinker of our times; that is why stupid people do him the honour to regard him as a public nuisance. *Saint Joan* reasserts his greatness.

CHAPTER V

The First Years : II. The Court Theatre

THE typical British creators are the comic writers. Shakespeare was, perhaps, not greater when he was creating Falstaff than when he was creating Hamlet, but he was certainly functioning more in accordance with the normal English genius. " A right pithy comedy " is its first printer's description of *Gammer Gurton's Needle*, and " right pithy " is a good phrase for the Cockney characters of Bernard Shaw. They are in the living tradition of the great comic writers, of Sterne and Smollett, and of Dickens, who alone has a richer and more varied portrait gallery of Londoners than Shaw. Yet Shaw's Cockneys occur in less than a third of his plays ! Burgess in *Candida*, Felix Drinkwater (of the " Worterloo Rowd ") in *Captain Brassbound*, 'Enry Straker, Rummy Mitchens and Snobby Price, 'Liza Doolittle and her father ! " Right pithy " indeed, and if none of them has the stature of Bill Crichton, that greatest Cockney of them all, it is certain that no dramatist since Ben Jonson has so diversely or divertingly reflected the London scene on the stage as Shaw. Which is, of course, merely one of his many strengths, and a result, quite possibly, of a minor preoccupation of his with dialect. His care for dialect is exhibited (besides in the dialogue) in the little disquisition on Cockney pronunciation in the opening stage directions of *Captain Brassbound's Conversion*, and, at fuller length, in the subject-matter of *Pygmalion*. It is open to anyone to object to the ideas in Shaw's plays—to think that they are wrong ideas or to think that there are too many ideas—but it is simply not open to think that Shaw hasn't a perfect feeling for, and a beautifully fastidious selection of, the right words. He 'speaks' to a miracle on the stage, and when the speaker is as right as the words he speaks—a Granville Barker as John Tanner or a Louis Calvert as Broadbent—the playgoer savours one of the keenest pleasures of the theatre.

Other of the Court dramatists had, if less genius, the same sedulous care for the right word. There were, as one has put it, intelligent interruptions to Shaw's hegemony at the Court, and there were a few interruptions which were less than intelligent. But the Court season, if it had found no new play except *The Silver Box*, would have justified itself. The plays of John Galsworthy are not *The Silver Box* and the rest; they are *The Silver Box*, *Strife*,

plays it shall be allowed its place along with (to recapitulate) the Gilbert Murray Euripides plays, *John Bull's Other Island*, *Man and Superman*, *Major Barbara*, *The Silver Box*, *The Voysey Inheritance*, and *Prunella*. It should be added that the Court did a play each by Ibsen, Maeterlinck, Hauptmann, and Schnitzler; but we are dealing here with the English renascence.

In those years of 1904–7 the Court had almost a monopoly of the great plays, but not quite, and the exception was the momentous one of *Peter Pan* in 1904. When Charles Lamb said that a man who refused apple dumplings couldn't have a pure mind, he stated the case for *Peter Pan*—which is not a comparison of that play with a dumpling, except on the ground that both are universal. It is not only the finest flower of the children's theatre —the notion that there ought to be a children's theatre at all belongs to this time—but, in the form of a masterly play and not in the formlessness of disjointed pictures, it is an almost uncannily profound exploration of the mind of a child. It is objective, with its skilled use of the visual resources of the stage, and it is also subjective in its imaginative beauty and its underlying profundity. Peter Pan himself is a real person for us all, as definitely established as Gulliver or Robinson Crusoe or Alice. One remembers the suggestion of some enthusiast during the Court Theatre season that Granville

Barker ought to be celebrated by his statue in Sloane Square, and it is possible to smile at that suggestion. We don't smile at any incongruity in the statue of Peter Pan in Kensington Gardens ; we couldn't wait till Peter Pan was dead ; he won't die, and he joins Bill Crichton as Barrie's chief contributions to the creations of the early years. Shaw has the larger gallery and the wider intellectual scope, but he has no individual creations of the stature of Bill Crichton and Peter Pan.

CHAPTER VI

John Brown's Soul

THE Court Theatre was not a financial success, except that the fact that it made nobody bankrupt may be regarded as a very great success for a three years' season of serious drama. But the partners, after working about sixteen hours a day for three years, closed the partnership and took out about £1500 each, which is not success as the theatrical speculator regards that word, and (considering the odds against him) has every right to regard it.

And if John Brown's body lay a-mouldering in the grave, his soul went marching on. What happened when the Court Theatre closed was the decentralization of serious drama and not its extinction. In London the aftermath of the Court was to be seen in the Kingsway management of Miss Lena Ashwell, in the Frohman Repertory season at the Duke of York's, in Granville Barker's managements, in the Vedrenne-Eadie Royalty Theatre management, in the Little Theatre management of Miss Gertrude Kingston followed by Mr Barker; generally by the peaceful penetration of the new

movement into the theatre at large, and par-
ticularly by the new phenomenon of the Abbey
Theatre in Dublin and the Repertory movement
in the English provinces.

Some of these enterprises were Court Theatre
and water—the new movement compromising with
the old, and the old asking itself if the new could
not be made to pay. Apart from Barrie, it hadn't
produced money for the theatre, but it had made
a serious breach in the money-producing poten-
tiality of the old drama. Sentimental melodrama,
for instance, had become no easy proposition. Since
the old Adelphi days melodrama had been dressing
itself in fine clothes, and the fine clothes of *The
Sign of the Cross* had helped, with its religious
motive, to make that play a tremendous success.
But by the time of *The Eternal City* religious
motive and fine clothes and His Majesty's Theatre
were among them all inadequate to conceal the
decline in the demand for melodrama, and even
the least sophisticated public was seen to have
acquired a new impatience with absurdity in the
theatre. Shaw hadn't laboured in vain, and the
die-hards of the old period were anxiously asking
themselves what was to be done about it; the
reply, obviously, was that they had better try some
of these strange new plays which didn't give
an actor-manager a fair chance of displaying his
mannerisms.

In the classic case of the young lady of Riga who went for a ride on a tiger there was no room for doubt as to which had swallowed the other ; and it might certainly seem, when both the Haymarket and His Majesty's Theatre surrendered to Bernard Shaw, that the new drama had swallowed the old ; but it has hardly done that. There was give and take, and there were adjustments on both sides, but the balance, up to the time of the War-theatre, was certainly on the side of the new movement ; then the pay of the colonial soldier effected the great reaction, from which we are only to-day emerging.

One of the less happy adjustments is to be in-stanced in the case of Hubert Henry Davies. The production in 1903 of *Cousin Kate* gave legitimate grounds for the hope that a new writer of comedy had arisen, but the actor-manager, either in the person of Sir Charles Wyndham, or the system of the actor-manager in general, captured Davies, who degenerated under the influence of the Star-who-must-be-served to the level of *Captain Drew on Leave* and *Mrs Epping's Law Suit*. Nothing so good as *Cousin Kate* succeeded that play, and Davies figures in one's compassionate regard as a victim of the actor-manager, always on the brink of first-rate comedy and never writing it. *The Mollusc* is a technical feat, not only in its economy of characters, but in its nice adjustment of the two chief parts to Charles Wyndham and Mary Moore. With them, it was delightful; without them, it is a thin little comedy. To use a word of the films, Davies was ' vamped ' by the actor-manager, and the point of him for our argument is that he illustrates the actor-managers' recognition of the necessity to adapt himself to the new spirit. Davies belonged with the new movement by virtue of his dialogue and his abhorrence of distortion; he belonged sufficiently with the old to make him easy prey. They say he died dissatisfied with his work, and, looking back, one feels he had it in him to write notable comedy. He surrendered, instead, to an actor-manager.

From another point of view Davies was of great value to the theatre; from the same point of view Mr Sutro and Mr Maugham are of great value. Theatres have to be kept open so that when works of theatrical art come along there shall be theatres in being to receive them. Professor Lyon Phelps says, with cruel candour, " An astonishingly successful dramatist like Somerset Maugham, for example, has had no influence at all; modern dramatic history would be the same if he had never written a play. In art it is always quality, not quantity, that counts." True, but a quantity of successful plays which may be less than art count very much in the important matter of keeping the theatres open : and whatever is to be thought of Mr Sutro's plays and Mr Maugham's, they are purged of the